Sports Illustrated KIDS

HOCKEY'S GREATEST

GAME-WINNING GOALS

AND OTHER CRUNCH-TIME HEROICS

BY THOM STORDEN

CAPSTONE PRESS
a capstone imprint

Captivate is published by Capstone Press, an imprint of Capstone.
1710 Roe Crest Drive, North Mankato, Minnesota 56003
www.capstonepub.com

**Library of Congress Cataloging-in-Publication Data is available on the Library
of Congress website.**
ISBN 978-1-4966-8732-6 (hardcover)
ISBN 978-1-4966-8740-1 (paperback)
ISBN 978-1-4966-8741-8 (ebook PDF)

Summary: When the pressure is on and a championship is at stake, some players
seize the moment and make themselves legends. From stunning breakaway goals
to jaw-dropping saves with only seconds left on the clock, some of hockey's greatest
moments are replayed vividly here. You've got a rink-side seat to the action.

Photo Credits
AP Photo: John Locher, 39; Getty Images: B Bennett, 13, 15, 17, 19, 36, Icon
Sportswire, 35, Len Redkoles, 7; Newscom: Icon Sportswire/Ken Murray, 29, KRT/
Nuccio Dinuzzo, 25, Reuters/David W Cerny, 5, Reuters/Mike Blake, 43, USA
Today Sports/Jeff Curry, 33; Shutterstock: Adam Vilimek, cover (rink), 1, dotshock,
cover (player), silvae, cover (lights), 1; Sports Illustrated: Damian Strohmeyer, 31,
David E. Klutho, 9, 41, Heinz Kluetmeier, 21, 23, Manny Millan, 45, Neil Leifer, 11,
Robert Beck, 26

Editorial Credits
Bobbie Nuytten, designer; Eric Gohl, media researcher; Katy LaVigne, production
specialist

TABLE OF CONTENTS

Words in **bold** are in the glossary.

THE CROWD GOES WILD

There's nothing like the sound of the crowd when a player scores a goal. When that goal is a game-winner? Even better! Maybe it's Patrick Kane or Sidney Crosby scoring a **clutch** goal in the Stanley Cup Finals. Maybe it's Marc-André Fleury or Patrick Roy with a clutch save. Or maybe it's an epic Olympic moment featuring the 1980 Americans or 1998 Czechs.

Clutch plays are plays made when the game—or the season—is on the line. Any serious hockey player or fan recognizes it. For heart-thumping, spine-tingling, glory-filled fun, there's nothing like a moment in the clutch.

Jocelyne Lamoureux-Davidson celebrates after scoring in a shootout in the gold-medal game between the U.S. and Canada.

CHAPTER 1

CLUTCH CUP MOMENTS

KANE'S CUP CLINCHER

The Chicago Blackhawks have been playing hockey a long time. Founded in 1926, the Blackhawks were one of the original six National Hockey League (NHL) teams. The Blackhawks won two Stanley Cup championships in their first 12 years. Then a long dry spell occurred. From 1938 to 1960, Chicago had only two winning seasons. Finally, in 1960–61 Chicago won its third-ever Stanley Cup.

Fast-forward nearly 50 years. The Blackhawks still hadn't won their fourth Stanley Cup. They'd gotten close. Five times they had lost in the championship. Blackhawks fans were getting restless.

Along came the 2009–10 Blackhawks. They sliced through the regular season and fought their way to the Stanley Cup Finals. They faced the Philadelphia Flyers. Chicago won the first two games. Philly came back to win the next two. Chicago won Game 5.

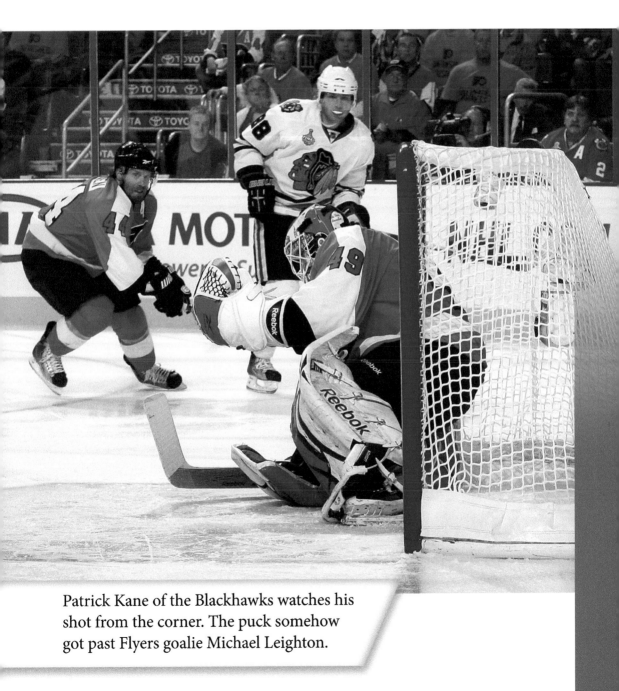

Patrick Kane of the Blackhawks watches his shot from the corner. The puck somehow got past Flyers goalie Michael Leighton.

Game 6 went into overtime tied at three. It was held in Philadelphia, and Flyers fans were fierce and loud. But with just over four minutes gone in overtime, Blackhawks right-winger Patrick Kane found himself with the puck. Kane had just one man to beat to get to the goalie. Putting a fake on his defender, Kane got free. Then he slapped a shot from a narrow angle to the side of the goal. Somehow, Kane's clutch shot whistled past the goalie. The rowdy crowd sat in stunned silence. Kane and his teammates skated the length of the ice in celebration. They couldn't believe that Kane's shot had gone in.

Kane and his teammates led the Blackhawks' return to greatness. In addition to winning the Cup in 2010, Chicago won it again in 2013 and 2015.

Patrick Kane was the first overall pick of the 2007 NHL Draft. He was born in Buffalo, New York, in 1988. That was the same year fellow Blackhawks star Jonathan Toews was born.

The Blackhawks celebrate their surprising victory after Kane's unlikely goal gave them a Stanley Cup championship.

THE ORIGINAL SIX

Beginning in 1942, the NHL had six original teams. These teams were the only six in the league until 1967.

1 Boston Bruins

2 Chicago Blackhawks

3 Detroit Red Wings

4 Montreal Canadiens

5 New York Rangers

6 Toronto Maple Leafs

THE GOAL

In the late 1960s and early 1970s, Bobby Orr was a hockey god. He was easily the best player in the NHL. This was before Wayne Gretzky came along and rewrote the record books. But Orr was truly special. Some still call him the best defensive player ever.

Orr turned pro in 1966. He was just 18 years old when he signed with the Boston Bruins. That season he won the Calder Trophy as the league's top rookie. The next season he won the Norris Trophy for best defender. This began a string of eight straight years of winning the Norris Trophy.

In 1969–70, Orr outdid himself. He won the Norris Trophy. He won the Ross Trophy (most individual points). He won the Hart Trophy (most valuable player). He won the Conn Smythe Trophy (most valuable player in the playoffs). All in the same season. No one had ever done that. No one has done it since.

Star defenseman Bobby Orr played 10 seasons for the Boston Bruins.

But Orr did something even more memorable than win awards in 1970. What many fans remember and still talk about is Orr's amazing Stanley Cup–winning shot. It is known simply as "The Goal."

Telling the story of The Goal involves lots of fours. It was Game 4 of the Stanley Cup Finals. It was the fourth period (overtime). Orr, who wore Bruins number 4, received a pass in front of the St. Louis Blues net. He took a shot. The shot broke a 3–3 tie, giving the Bruins their fourth goal of the game. With the win, the Bruins swept the Blues, 4–0. It gave the Bruins a fourth Stanley Cup title.

But what, in part, made the shot so **legendary** was a photo. Shot by Ray Lussier, the photo shows hockey glory at its peak. It depicts Orr flying through the air, having just scored the winning goal. With Orr's arms outstretched in victory, the Boston crowd goes wild in the background.

Some say that a Blues defender tripped Orr. Some say Orr took a victory leap. It doesn't really matter. It's an amazing photo of an amazing moment.

Bobby Orr led Boston to two Stanley Cup victories, in 1970 and 1972. It would be 38 seasons until the Bruins won the Stanley Cup again in 2011.

A famous photo captured Orr's leap for joy after scoring a tie-breaking goal in the Stanley Cup Finals.

LUSSIER'S HUSTLE

Photographer Ray Lussier might not have gotten the famous photo of Bobby Orr's Superman dive if he hadn't been on his toes. Lussier was given a press pass at the east end of the arena. The west end was where the Bruins would be attacking in overtime. Lussier hustled. He found an empty spot. The person assigned the spot had gone to get a beer during intermission. Just 40 seconds into overtime, Lussier got his picture. The Bruins unveiled a statue of "The Shot" in 2010.

COMEBACK KINGS

No one likes to be embarrassed.

The Los Angeles Kings fell behind, 5–0, in an important 1982 NHL playoff game. During the break between the second and third periods, Kings players were ashamed. They noticed some things. The opponents, the Edmonton Oilers, were laughing. Oilers players were pointing at the scoreboard. They gave the Kings no respect.

But that would change.

The Kings scored two quick goals to open the final period. Then they scored two more. The score was 5–4. The Kings fans who had stayed in L.A.'s arena past the second period woke up. The Oilers and their stars, Wayne Gretzky and Mark Messier, clung to the lead. With five seconds left, the Kings scored on Oilers goalie Grant Fuhr. The arena erupted.

In overtime, the Kings completed the comeback. Rookie Daryl Evans put the winning goal in the net, past Fuhr. Evans happily sped down the ice in celebration. Afterward, his name was announced as the first star of the game. Said Evans, "It seemed like I was skating on air."

Daryl Evans led the L.A. Kings against Wayne Gretzky and the high-powered Edmonton Oilers.

The Kings beat the Oilers three games to two to win the series. They lost in the next round of the playoffs. The New York Islanders won the 1982 Stanley Cup.

GAME 7 STUNNER

The Detroit Red Wings were facing the New York Rangers in the 1950 Stanley Cup Finals. The Red Wings had the best record in the league. They were led by Sid Abel, Ted Lindsay, and Gordie Howe.

This was the first time in seven years that two American teams would face off for the Cup. The Stanley Cup games, however, were not all played in the United States. The Rangers' home, Madison Square Garden, was being rented out by a traveling circus. So the Rangers chose Toronto as their temporary home. Toronto had won the previous three Cups. There were plenty of hockey fans there.

The Rangers and Red Wings split the first six games. A final seventh game would decide the winner. It was only the third time the Stanley Cup Finals had gone seven games. Game 7, played in Detroit, was hard-fought. The game went into overtime. And then double overtime. Finally, Pete Babando knocked in the game-winning, Cup-winning goal. Detroit would go on to win three more Cups in the 1950s.

Pete Babando was born in Pennsylvania in 1925. He was the only 1949–50 Red Wings player who was born in the U.S. Nearly all of the Red Wings players had been born in Canada.

Detroit's Jim McFadden (third from left) got a shot past New York goalie Chuck Rayner in the 1950 Stanley Cup Finals.

MAPLE LEAFS LEGEND

The Toronto Maple Leafs faced the Montreal Canadiens for the Stanley Cup. It was 1951. The Maple Leafs had won the Cup five times in the 1940s. So they knew how to win it all. The Maple Leafs had great players. One of those players was Bill Barilko. In 1951, the 24-year-old **defenseman** was just making a name for himself.

The first four games of the 1951 Cup had all gone into overtime. Toronto had won three. One more victory would secure the Cup. Game 5 was another close one. It went into overtime. With the score tied at two, Barilko broke the tie with a game-winning goal and gave the Maple Leafs the Cup. Toronto fans were on top of the world.

All the excitement soon came crashing down. Four months after his game-winner, Barilko vanished. He went on a fishing trip and was flying in a plane with a friend, but the plane disappeared. A long search turned up nothing. Finally, in 1962, the wreckage of the plane and the remains of Barilko and the others were found in a Canadian forest. It is not known exactly why the plane crashed, but finding it gave closure to the mystery. Strangely, the Maple Leafs had recently won the Cup again for the first time since Barilko's goal.

Bill Barilko goes to the ice as his shot gets past goalie Gerry McNeil in Game 5 of the 1951 Stanley Cup Finals.

A famous Canadian rock band named The Tragically Hip wrote a song about Barilko. The song is called "Fifty Mission Cap." It is regularly played before Maple Leafs games.

CHAPTER 2

OLYMPIC HEROICS

MIRACULOUS

Some sports moments are so epic that they leave people wanting more. That is one reason why players and fans alike enjoy sharing memories of special moments, games, and seasons. Some folks do other things to honor the memories. They paint pictures. They create songs. They build statues. They write stories. And if a sports moment is really special, it's turned into a movie.

The movie *Miracle* came out in 2004. It tells the story of the 1980 U.S. Olympic men's hockey team and their coach, Herb Brooks. The Soviet Union had what was thought to be an unbeatable squad, and the Americans bested them. The movie starred Kurt Russell as Brooks, the tough but crafty coach. It went on to become one of the best-known hockey movies of all time.

When events in the movie happened in real life at the 1980 Olympics, it was nearly unbelievable. The Soviets had an incredible team. They beat the Americans, 10–3, in an exhibition game just two weeks before the Olympics started.

U.S. goalie Jim Craig played heroically in the 1980 Olympics.

But once the Games got underway, the Americans clicked. Goaltender Jim Craig became a brick wall in the net. Team captain Mike Eruzione played the best hockey of his life. Team USA met the Soviets in the semifinals. The Soviets started fast. They took a 2–1 lead. Then, just as the first period was about to end, the Americans scored. Tie game.

Angry, the Soviet coach pulled his starting goalie, Vladislav Tretiak. The coach put in Vladimir Myshkin. The Soviets scored another goal to take a 3–2 lead. But the Americans would not give up. Jim Craig made plenty of saves, and the Americans tied it up again on a David Silk goal. Then, not two minutes later, the Americans struck again. This time it was Mike Eruzione, on a 25-foot slapshot.

The American-heavy crowd went wild. The U.S. held on. But after the big win, the Americans had one more important game. The gold-medal game. They played tough hockey and came out on top, beating Finland. Many call the U.S. victory over the Soviets the biggest underdog win of all time.

Mike Eruzione never played in the NHL. Also, the 1980 Olympics ended his career on the U.S. team.

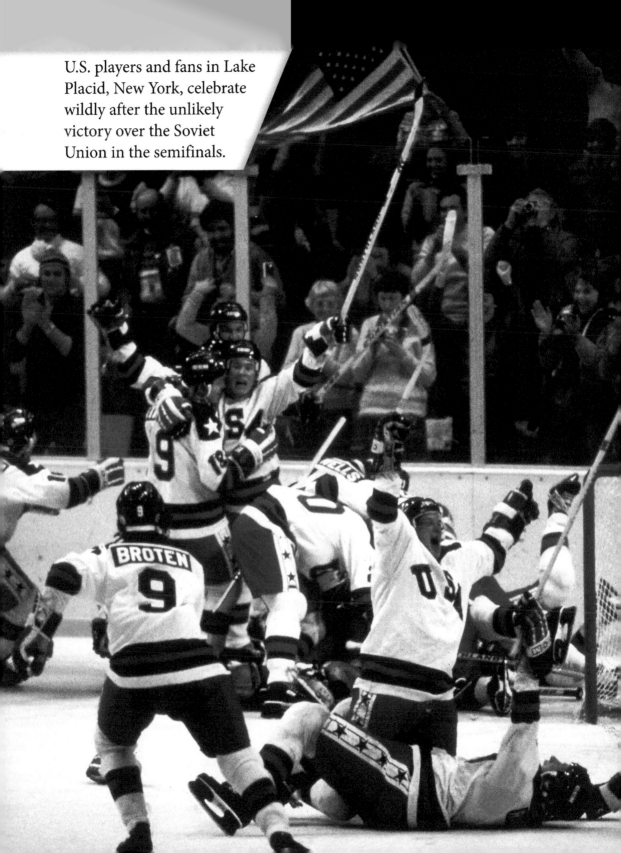

U.S. players and fans in Lake Placid, New York, celebrate wildly after the unlikely victory over the Soviet Union in the semifinals.

CZECH DOMINATION

For the first time in Olympic history, the NHL took a break during the 1998 Games. This meant that all pro players could represent their countries in the Olympics. As a result, the level of hockey at the 1998 Nagano, Japan, Games was expected to be very high.

Czechoslovakia went through great change in the early 1990s. In 1993, the country split in two, forming Slovakia and the Czech Republic. One thing that had not changed was that Czech hockey players remained very talented. Before the 1998 Olympics, Czechoslovakia had medaled eight times but never won gold.

In the quarterfinals, the Czechs breezed by the U.S., 4–1. Then they took on Canada. Canada was considered the tournament favorite. They had stars such as Wayne Gretzky and Eric Lindros. They had Patrick Roy and Martin Brodeur in goal. They were some of the greatest players of all time.

But the Czechs had a young player named Jaromír Jágr. They had Petr Svoboda. And they had goalie Dominik Hašek. Hašek was nicknamed "The Dominator," and he was at the top of his game. He was the most recent Hart Trophy winner in the NHL.

The game between Canada and the Czech Republic was tight. The Czechs finally scored in the third period and then tried to hold on. But Canada finally tied the game, 1–1, with about a minute left. An overtime period produced no goals.

The game went to a **shootout**. The Czechs' first shooter, Robert Reichel, scored on Canada's Roy. That would be all the Czechs needed. Five Canadians took their best shot. Hašek didn't let a single puck into the net. The Czechs won. The Canadians were in disbelief.

In the gold-medal game, Hašek continued his great play. He completely stonewalled Russia. Hašek did not allow a single goal. The Czech Republic won, 1–0. They had captured the gold.

Dominik Hašek was an NHL star when he helped his home country to an Olympic victory.

GOLDEN GIRL

Marie-Philip Poulin does her best work when it matters most.

At the 2010 Olympics in Vancouver, Canada, Poulin was just 18 years old. She had just made Canada's senior women's national team the year before. Team Canada was rewarded for choosing her when she scored— twice!—in the 2010 Olympic gold-medal game. In fact, Poulin's two goals were the only ones scored. Canada beat the United States, 2–0. It was a great win for the team.

Canada's Marie-Philip Poulin scored twice in the Olympic finals and helped her team claim the gold.

Four years later, the Winter Games were held in Russia. Poulin struck again. In the final game to decide the 2014 gold-medal winner, Poulin again scored twice. Again facing the U.S. This time, her goals were even more dramatic. Her first goal tied the game with less than a minute left. Her second won it in overtime.

Poulin said, "Those are the moments you work for. That's why I'm in the gym every day. That's why I'm on the ice. You want to play in those big moments."

BEST OF THE BEST

Since women's hockey was introduced in 1998 as an Olympic sport, Canada has dominated. Here is a complete list of women's Olympic hockey medal-winning teams.

YEAR	GOLD	SILVER	BRONZE
1998	USA	Canada	Finland
2002	Canada	USA	Sweden
2006	Canada	Sweden	USA
2010	Canada	USA	Finland
2014	Canada	USA	Switzerland
2018	USA	Canada	Finland

BREAKING THROUGH

The U.S.-Canada women's hockey **rivalry** was **competitive**. In 1998 they met in the first women's hockey Olympic gold-medal game. The U.S. came out on top with a 3–1 victory. Canada went on to capture gold in the next four winter Games. The U.S. finished runner-up in three of those four Games.

But 2018 felt different for the American women. A number of the players had played through losses to Canada in 2010 and 2014. Among them were twin sisters Jocelyne Lamoureux-Davidson and Monique Lamoureux-Morando.

The U.S. and Canada both made it to the final with strong play. The game was tied at one goal apiece when Canadian star Marie-Philip Poulin scored to give Canada the lead. The U.S. would not give up. They tied the score 2–2 on a goal by Monique Lamoureux-Morando. The game went into overtime. The overtime was scoreless. The winner would have to be decided by shootout.

After five shots each, the score remained tied. Then American winger Jocelyne Lamoureux-Davidson scored. All the U.S. had to do was stop one puck. That's just what U.S. goalie Maddie Rooney did. After 20 years, the Americans had again captured gold.

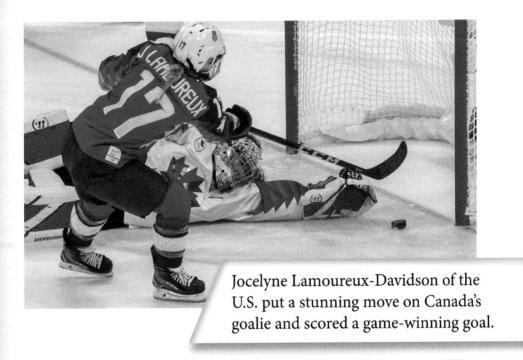

Jocelyne Lamoureux-Davidson of the U.S. put a stunning move on Canada's goalie and scored a game-winning goal.

PUCK PIONEERS

For the first time in history, an Asian team won hockey gold in January 2020. Playing in the 2020 Youth Winter Games in Switzerland, Japan took the gold in women's ice hockey. They downed two-time reigning champions Sweden 4–1 in the final.

THE GOLDEN GOAL

It was the final day of the 2010 Winter Olympics. Canada and the United States were prepared to face off for the gold medal in men's hockey. Fans filed into the arena in Vancouver, where the Games took place.

A week earlier, the U.S. had bested Canada in an opening-round game. But the two teams fought through the medal round to meet in the final. Canada went up 2–0 before the Americans rallied. First the U.S.'s Ryan Kesler scored. Then, with just 24 seconds left in the third period, Zach Parise scored. The game went into overtime.

The Americans' goalie, Ryan Miller, hung tough. He made some great clutch saves, as he had all tournament long. Finally, with nearly eight minutes gone in overtime, Canada's Jerome Iginla flicked a pass to Sidney Crosby. Crosby had recently led his NHL team, the Pittsburgh Penguins, to the Stanley Cup title. Crosby stormed the goal from the left side. He slapped a shot.

Goal!

Crosby's shot became known as "The Golden Goal." The arena went crazy. The home team had done it.

Canada's Sidney Crosby (87) in the gold-medal game against the U.S.

Sidney Crosby helped Canada win a second consecutive gold in the 2014 Olympics. He was born in Halifax, Nova Scotia, in eastern Canada.

CHAPTER 3

SUPER SAVES

SAVING ST. LOUIS

Sports fans love it when a player seems to have come from out of nowhere. Jordan Binnington is one of these players. He was always talented. But he wasn't a super-fast learner. The goalie was a third-round pick for the St. Louis Blues in 2011. For years he played in the minor leagues.

During that time, Binnington grew older. But he did not always grow wiser. Some of his habits were lazy. His desire to make it as a pro was questioned. But something changed in Binnington. He began to work harder. He changed his training methods. He lifted weights more seriously, practiced harder. He paid attention.

In December of 2018 the Blues called him up from the minors. Days before, the Blues' record was the worst in the league. In Binnington's first start in goal, he led his team to a 3–0 **shutout** over the Philadelphia

Flyers. Binnington did not let up. He finished the season with a 24–5 record in goal. His 1.89 goals-against average was the best in the league.

The Blues made the playoffs. Binnington was their anchor. He was key to every win of the Blues' postseason. The Blues won the Cup, and they wouldn't have done it without Binnington.

Jordan Binnington in action for the Blues

DOUBLE CLUTCH

The playoffs. Late in the third and final period. Score tied at three. The puck sliding past the goalie. Heading for the net . . .

Saved!

It was Game 7 in a 2019 playoff matchup between the Carolina Hurricanes and Washington Capitals. The season was on the line for both teams. The loser would go home. The Capitals' Tom Wilson had passed to his teammate, Niklas Bäckström. But the puck was blocked by Hurricanes goalie Petr Mrázek.

But Mrázek lost sight of the blocked puck. To the Hurricanes' horror, it was heading right for the goal. That's when the Hurricanes' Brock McGinn came through. Pouncing like a cat, he dove behind his goalie. Just in the nick of time, he knocked the puck away.

The game went into overtime. Then double overtime. McGinn's clutch effort wasn't finished. At the 11:05 mark of double overtime, McGinn scored the winning goal. His double-duty heroics saved the season.

McGinn and the Hurricanes nearly made it to the Stanley Cup Finals. They were stopped by the Boston Bruins in the semifinals. The St. Louis Blues beat Boston to win it all in 2019.

Brock McGinn (23) stretches to help his goalie and prevent the Capitals from scoring.

WORKING OVERTIME

Patrick Roy always gave his all in the NHL. Over 19 seasons. Over 1,029 regular season games. Over another 247 playoff games. But the goalie may have done his finest work in the 1993 playoffs.

Roy's team, the Montreal Canadiens, finished 48–30–6 in 1992–93. They played the favored Quebec Nordiques in the opening round of the playoffs. In the first game, Roy and Montreal lost in overtime, 3–2.

Patrick Roy helped his team win four straight games in the 1993 Stanley Cup Finals.

In Game 2, Montreal lost again. But that's when Roy went to work. He dug deeper. Roy and the Canadiens won the next four games straight, two in overtime.

Then the Canadiens beat the Buffalo Sabres in four straight—three in overtime. After the Canadiens beat the New York Islanders in the first three games of the semifinals (two in overtime), that made 11 straight wins. Roy was on fire.

Montreal closed out New York then faced the L.A. Kings for the Stanley Cup. They lost Game 1. But then Roy took over. The Canadiens won four in a row—three in overtime—to clinch the Cup. In 11 overtime playoff games, Roy won 10 straight and gave up only one goal. That's a job well done.

Patrick Roy won four Stanley Cups. He won two with the Montreal Canadiens and two with the Colorado Avalanche.

PRETTY GOOD

Marc-André Fleury has made his share of saves at the net. The goalie came into the NHL with the Pittsburgh Penguins in 2003. He was just 18 years old. But he was a puck-stopper extraordinaire. In his first game, he stopped 46 shots. In his first month, he recorded a shutout. He helped the Penguins to Stanley Cups in 2009, 2016, and 2017.

In 2017–18 Fleury joined the Vegas Golden Knights. They were an expansion franchise. But they were very good. So good, in fact, that they made it to the Stanley Cup Finals. Though they lost in the championship, it was Fleury who drove their success.

Fleury's last name is close to the French word for flower—Fleury means "in bloom." Often, the goalie has displayed flower-like artwork on his mask. He regularly sports the fleur-de-lis, a famous French symbol. For many years, Pittsburgh fans marveled at Fleury's pretty saves.

In a game in 2019, Fleury reminded fans why he's so great. Playing the Toronto Maple Leafs, Vegas led 3–2 late in the game. A Leafs player slapped a shot off the crossbar. The rebound went right to another Leafs player, who fired again. Caught out too far from the net, Fleury dove. Amazingly, he snared the puck in his glove. Just another pretty save in the career of Marc-André Fleury.

Marc-André Fleury dives to make an amazing glove save.

CHAPTER 4

LEGENDS OF CRUNCH TIME

CLUTCH IN THE PLAYOFFS

Most hockey fans point to Wayne Gretzky as the greatest hockey player of all time. But was he the best clutch player? Well, what defines *clutch*? Certainly playing at one's best in the biggest games matters. So what are the biggest games? Playoffs, right? Stanley Cup Finals? For sure.

Two players share the record for most playoff game–winning goals at 24. Those players are Wayne Gretzky and Brett Hull. But that might be where the similarities between the two great scorers end. Four of Gretzky's 24 game-winners came in overtime. Only one of Hull's did. But Hull's single overtime game-winner won the Stanley Cup. None of Gretzky's overtime winners did that.

In 1999 Hull's Cup-winner came while he was a member of the Dallas Stars. He did it in triple overtime versus the Buffalo Sabres. It was Game 6 and both teams were worn out. They had played

Brett Hull rips a shot on goal.

nearly two full games of hockey. But some said Hull's goal should not have counted. His foot was in the **crease**. But the officials ruled that it was legal.

While Hull won the Cup just once, Gretzky won the Stanley Cup four times. Each time he did it as a member of the Edmonton Oilers.

PLAYOFF GOALS

Most Goals Scored in the Playoffs, Career

	PLAYER	GOALS	TEAMS
1	Wayne Gretzky	122	Oilers, Kings, Blues, Rangers
2	Mark Messier	109	Oilers, Rangers
3	Jari Kurri	106	Oilers, Kings, Rangers, Ducks, Avalanche
4	Brett Hull	103	Flames, Blues, Stars, Red Wings
5	Glenn Anderson	93	Oilers, Maple Leafs, Rangers, Blues

CLUTCH CONN SMYTH WINNERS

The most valuable player in the Stanley Cup playoffs wins the Conn Smythe Trophy. Only three players in pro hockey history have won it two seasons in a row. Philadelphia Flyers goalie Bernie Parent did it first. He won it in 1974 and 1975. Mario Lemieux of the Pittsburgh Penguins did it in 1991 and 1992. And Sidney Crosby, also of the Penguins, did it in 2016 and 2017.

During Parent's back-to-back wins, he put up 30 shutouts. He may have dominated for longer if not for a neck injury and then a career-ending eye injury in 1979.

Lemieux is considered one of the most talented hockey players ever. In the playoffs in 1991 and 1992, Lemieux scored an amazing 78 points in 38 games. The Penguins won the Cup both years. He holds the mark for highest playoff goals per game with 0.71.

Crosby overcame injuries to find glory. Early in his career, he sustained many **concussions**. For three seasons straight starting in 2010–11, he missed at least half the season due to injuries. But he came back. He led Pittsburgh to the Cup in 2016. In 2017 he set the Penguins' record, passing Lemieux, for most points (20) in a Stanley Cup Final.

Mario Lemieux celebrates after he and the Penguins defeated the Minnesota North Stars for the Stanley Cup.

Conn Smythe owned the Toronto Maple Leafs from 1927 to 1961. He served in World War I and World War II. He was also a racehorse owner, and he was known for his charity.

STANLEY CUP TRIVIA

In hockey, nothing is more clutch than winning the Stanley Cup in a best-of-seven games series. See if you can get the right answers to these seven brain-busting Stanley Cup trivia questions.

1. What was the original name of the Stanley Cup?

A. Highest Hockey Honors In the Land Contest

B. The Excelsior Crown

C. Dominion Hockey Challenge Cup

D. Lord Vader Trophy Cup

2. Why was the 1919 Stanley Cup Finals canceled?

A. World War I

B. The Great Vancouver Flood

C. Player protest

D. Spanish Flu pandemic

3. What franchise has the most Stanley Cup titles?

A. Toronto Maple Leafs

B. Montreal Canadiens

C. Chicago Blackhawks

D. Colorado Avalanche

4. Which player has won the Conn Smyth Trophy (Stanley Cup Finals MVP) a record number of three times?

A. Patrick Roy

B. Wayne Gretzky

C. Maurice Richard

D. Gordie Howe

5. Which team captured the Stanley Cup by getting all four of its wins in overtime?

A. 1951 Toronto Maple Leafs

B. 1985 Edmonton Oilers

C. 1999 Dallas Stars

D. 2016 Pittsburgh Penguins

6. Who was the first American-born player to win the Conn Smythe Trophy?

A. Neal Broten

B. Patrick Kane

C. Brian Leetch

D. Jonathan Quick

7. Who won the longest game in Stanley Cup history?

A. Edmonton Oilers

B. Vancouver Canucks

C. New York Rangers

D. Minnesota North Stars

Wayne Gretzky (99) led the Edmonton Oilers to several Stanley Cup championships in the 1980s, and he still holds NHL records for goals and points in a career.

Answers: 1-C; 2-D, 3-B (24 times); 4-A(1986, 1993, 2001); 5-A; 6-C; 7-A (defeated Bruins 3-2 Game 1, 1990, 15:13 into 3rd OT)

GLOSSARY

clutch (KLUTCH)—done in an important situation or under great pressure

competitive (kuhm-PET-i-tiv)—very eager to win, succeed, or excel

concussion (kuhn-KUH-shuhn)—an injury to the brain caused by a hard blow to the head

crease (KREES)—the area directly in front of the goal in hockey; it's often painted blue

defenseman (dih-FENS-muhn)—a player who lines up in a defensive zone to prevent opponents from getting open shots on goal

legendary (LEJ-uhnd-air-ee)—something or someone that is well-known or famous

rivalry (RYE-val-ree)—a fierce feeling of competition between two people or teams

shootout (SHOOT-out)—a shooting competition in overtime that is used to determine the winner of a game (as in soccer or hockey) that is tied at the end of regular play

shutout (SHUHT-out)—to keep an opposing team from scoring

READ MORE

McCollum, Sean. *Hockey's Best and Worst*. North Mankato, MN: Capstone Press, 2018.

Omoth, Tyler. *A Superfan's Guide to Pro Hockey Teams*. North Mankato, MN: Capstone Press, 2018.

Savage, Jeff. *Hockey Super Stats*. Minneapolis: Lerner Publications, 2017.

INTERNET SITES

Hockey Hall of Fame
www.hhof.com

Hockey Reference
www.hockey-reference.com

National Hockey League
www.nhl.com

SOURCE NOTES

p. 14, "It seemed like I . . ." John Kreiser, "Most Memorable Moments in Kings History," NHL.com, https://www.nhl.com/news/most-memorable-moments-in-kings-history/c-282631322 Accessed April 3, 2020.

p. 27, "Those are the moments . . ." Michelle Crechiolo, "Marie-Philip Poulin: Captain Clutch," NHL.com, nhl.com/penguins/news/marie-philip-poulin-captain-clutch-team-canada/c-311133424 Accessed March 18, 2020.

INDEX